PIANO · VOCAL · GUITAR

TURNING RED: MUSIC FROM THE MOTION PICTURE SOUNDTRACK

ORIGINAL SONGS BY **BILLIE EILISH** AND **FINNEAS O'CON...**
ORIGINAL SCORE BY **LUDWIG GÖRANSSON**

Meilin Lee

STUDENT

Lester B. Pearson
Middle School
2002-2003

Disney · PIXAR

TURNING RED

ISBN 978-1-70516-913-1

HAL·LEONARD®

Visit Hal Leonard Online at
www.halleonard.com

World headquarters, contact:
Hal Leonard
7777 West Bluemound Road
Milwaukee, WI 53213
Email: info@halleonard.com

In Europe, contact:
Hal Leonard Europe Limited
42 Wigmore Street
Marylebone, London, W1U 2RY
Email: info@halleonardeurope.com

In Australia, contact:
Hal Leonard Australia Pty. Ltd.
4 Lentara Court
Cheltenham, Victoria, 3192 Australia
Email: info@halleonard.com.au

CONTENTS

9 **NOBODY LIKE U**

18 **1 TRUE LOVE**

24 **U KNOW WHAT'S UP**

15 **TURNING RED**

29 **TEMPLE DUTIES**

30 **PANDA-MONIUM**

34 **KEEPING THE PANDA**

33 **RED MOON RITUAL**

36 **MAKING IT RIGHT**

38 **LET YOUR INNER PANDA OUT**

NOBODY LIKE U

Music and Lyrics by BILLIE EILISH
and FINNEAS O'CONNELL

Moderate groove

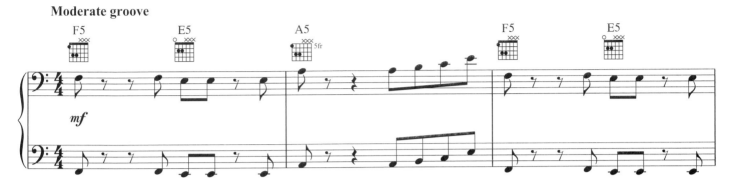

I've nev-er met no-bod-y ___ like ___ you. Had friends and I've had

bud-dies, ___ it's ___ true. ___ But they don't turn my tum-my ___ the way ___ you ___

do. I've nev-er met no-bod-y like _____ you, oh.

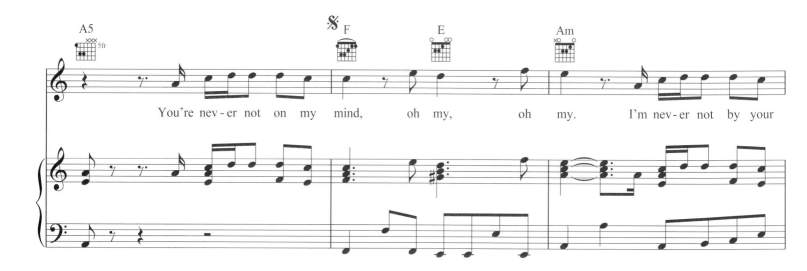

You're nev-er not on my mind, oh my, oh my. I'm nev-er not by your

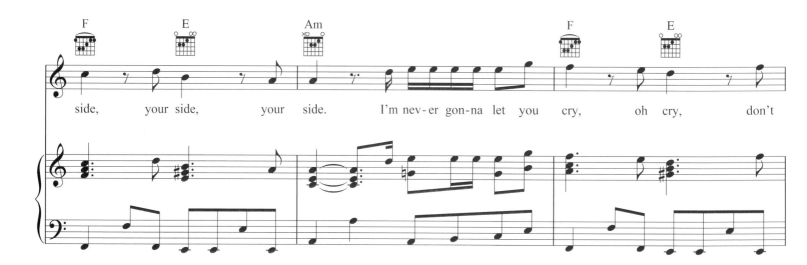

side, your side, your side. I'm nev-er gon-na let you cry, oh cry, don't

ev - 'ry - bod - y to stop and stare, _ and you know why. It's me, Ro - baire.

Woo, uhh, let's

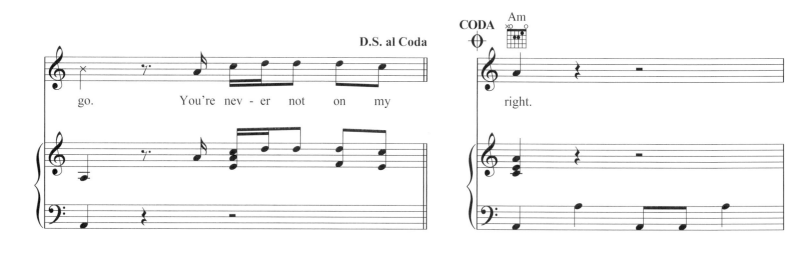

D.S. al Coda

go. You're nev - er not on my

CODA Am

right.

N.C.

Li, li, li, li, li, like you. Li, li, li, li, li, like you.

Li, li, li, li, li, like you. Like __ you, like __ you.

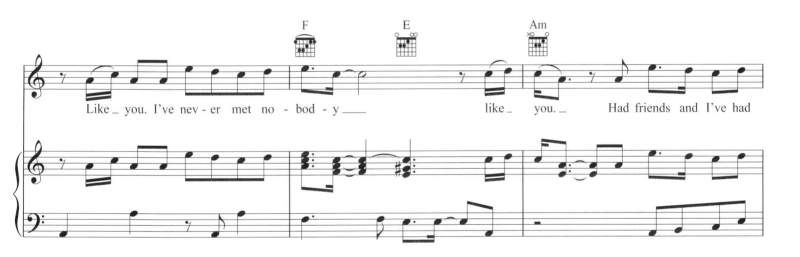

Li, li, li, li, li, like you. Li, li, li, li, li, like you. Li, li, li, li, __ like __ you.

Like __ you. I've nev - er met no - bod - y __ like __ you. __ Had friends and I've had

bud - dies, __ it's _____ true. But they don't turn my tum - my _____ the way __ you __

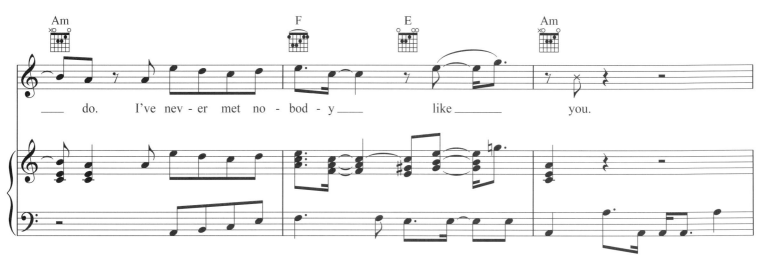

do. I've nev-er met no-bod-y ____ like ____ you.

You're nev-er not on my mind, oh my, oh my. I'm nev-er not by your

side, your side, your side. I'm nev-er gon-na let you cry, oh cry, don't

cry. ____ I'll nev-er not be your ride or die, al-right.

TURNING RED

Composed by
LUDWIG GÖRANSSON

1 TRUE LOVE

Music and Lyrics by BILLIE EILISH
and FINNEAS O'CONNELL

(Ooh, _____ yeah, _____ yeah.) _____

Heav-y rain _____ from my cloud-y eyes, _____ ev'-ry time you say _____ that it is-n't wise _____

_____ to call you babe. _____ But you're the light of my life. _____

I drove by your house _____ twen-ty-nine

times to-day. No - bod - y else ___ could make me

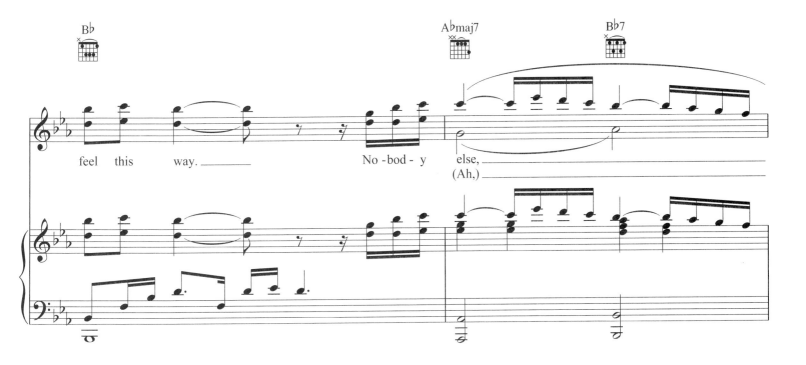

feel this way. ___ No - bod - y else, ___
(Ah,) ___

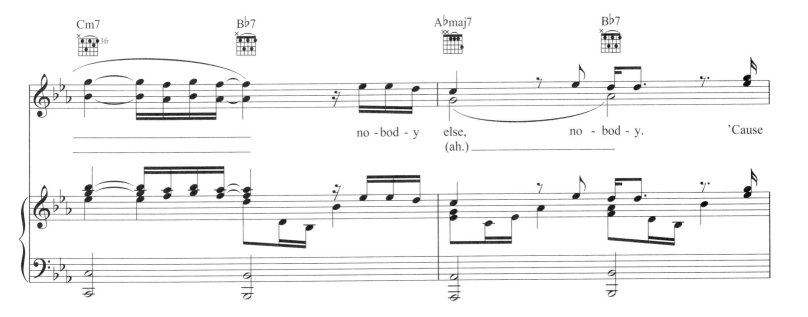

no - bod - y else, no - bod - y. 'Cause
(ah.)

you've o - pened my eyes ___ and sto - len my heart. ___ You make me be - lieve ___ that love ___ can be hard, ___

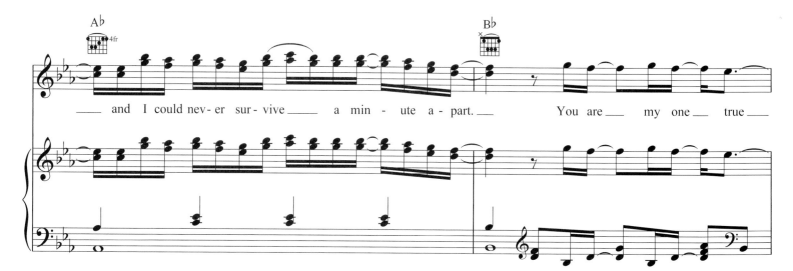

___ and I could nev - er sur - vive ___ a min - ute a - part. ___ You are ___ my one ___ true ___

___ love, my one ___ true ___ love. My heav - en a - bove, ___

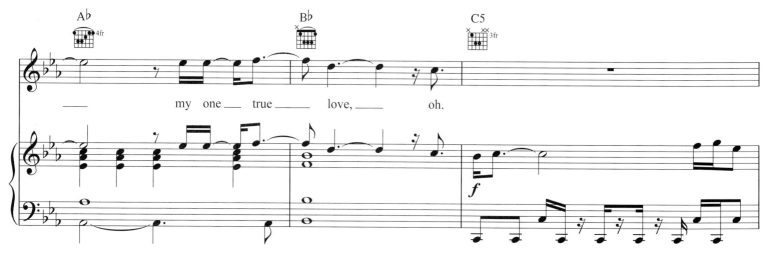

___ my one ___ true ___ love, ___ oh.

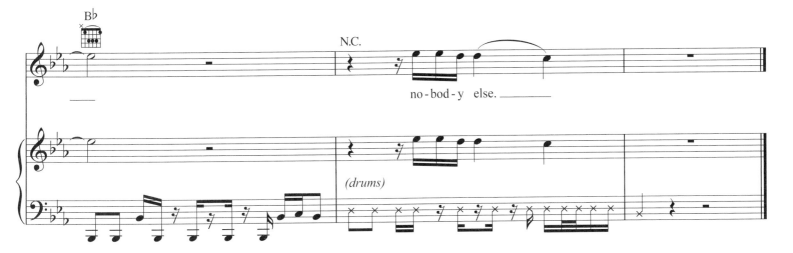

U KNOW WHAT'S UP

Music and Lyrics by BILLIE EILISH
and FINNEAS O'CONNELL

Moderate Pop groove

I'm gon-na make it all the way, just watch me. I'm gon-na hus-tle ev-'ry

day, ____ oh. _____ I'm mak-ing pa-per like it's o - ri - ga - mi.

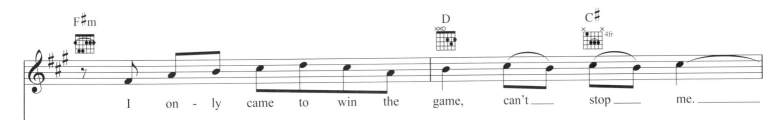

I on-ly came to win the game, can't ____ stop ____ me. _____

____ You want - ed it, you went __ for it, and ba - by, you got it.

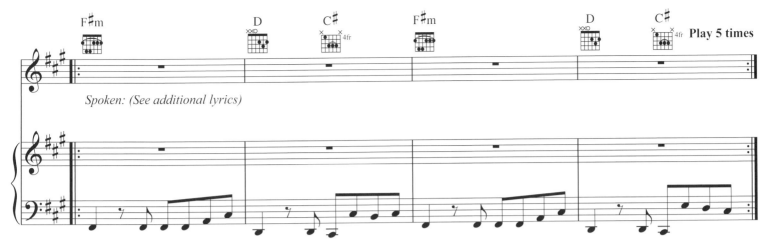

Spoken: (See additional lyrics)

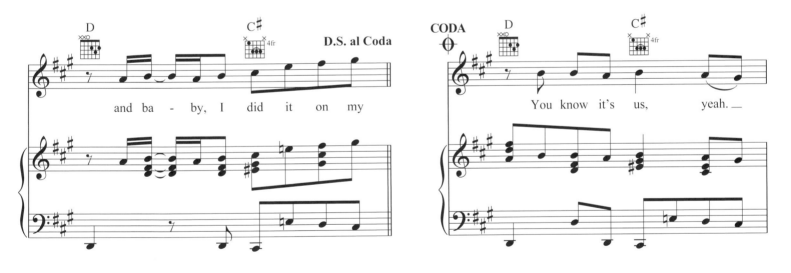

You want - ed it, you went __ for it, and ba - by, you got it. I want - ed it, I went __ for it,

and ba - by, I did it on my

CODA

You know it's us, yeah. __

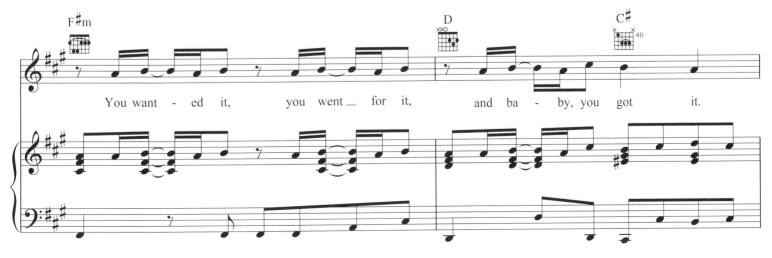

You want - ed it, you went __ for it, and ba - by, you got it.

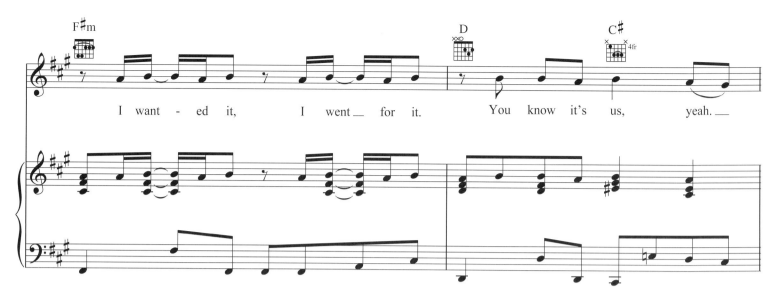

Additional Lyrics

Spoken: Ladies and gentlemen, listen up.
I'm gonna ask you a few questions and I just want you to be honest with me.
You want those shoes?
You want that shirt?
You want that car?
You want that purse?
Huh, I'm gonna need you to convince me.
You ready?
Here we go.
You want it?
I want it.
You want it?
I want it.
You want it?
I want it.
Louder.
You want it?
I want it.
You want it?
I want it.
You want it?
I want it.
Give me one, two, three, four!

TEMPLE DUTIES

Composed by
LUDWIG GÖRANSSON

PANDA-MONIUM

Composed by
LUDWIG GÖRANSSON

Moderately fast

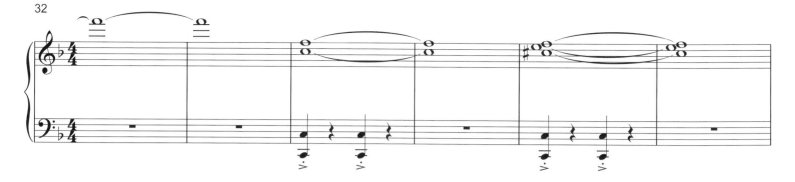

Pedal ad lib.

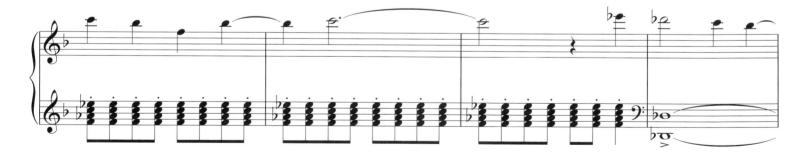

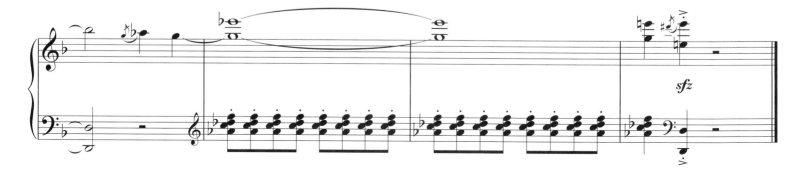

sfz

RED MOON RITUAL

Composed by
LUDWIG GÖRANSSON

Moderately

KEEPING THE PANDA

Composed by
LUDWIG GÖRANSSON

Moderately, steadily

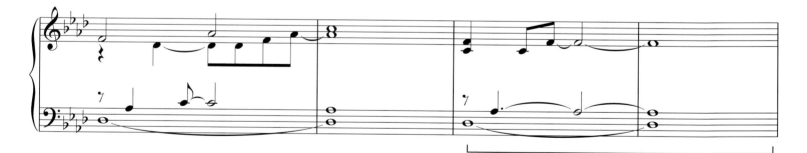

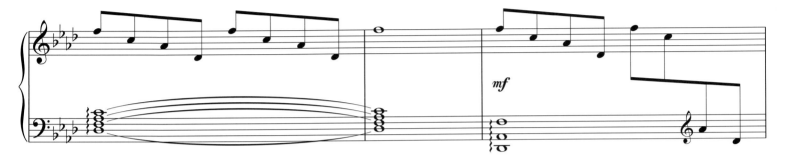

MAKING IT RIGHT

Composed by
LUDWIG GÖRANSSON

Half as fast

LET YOUR INNER PANDA OUT

Composed by
LUDWIG GÖRANSSON

Moderately